ALPHABET animals
COLORING BOOK

52 different ANIMALS

BY JOY KELLEY

All artwork in this coloring book was created by Joy Kelley of HowJoyful LLC.

HowJoyful is a trademark registered in the United States.
For comments or questions, please contact us via email:
hello@howjoyful.com

Published by HowJoyful LLC
ISBN: 978-1-7330369-5-5
Second Edition: September 2022

NOTE: The author has no oversight over the printing process or paper quality, and while this paper is suited for crayons and color pencils, it's not the best for markers. We have set a dark gray page in the back of each coloring page to help with the color bleeding and see-through.

www.howjoyful.com/books

this book
IS FOR

with love
FROM

lowercase alphabet reference

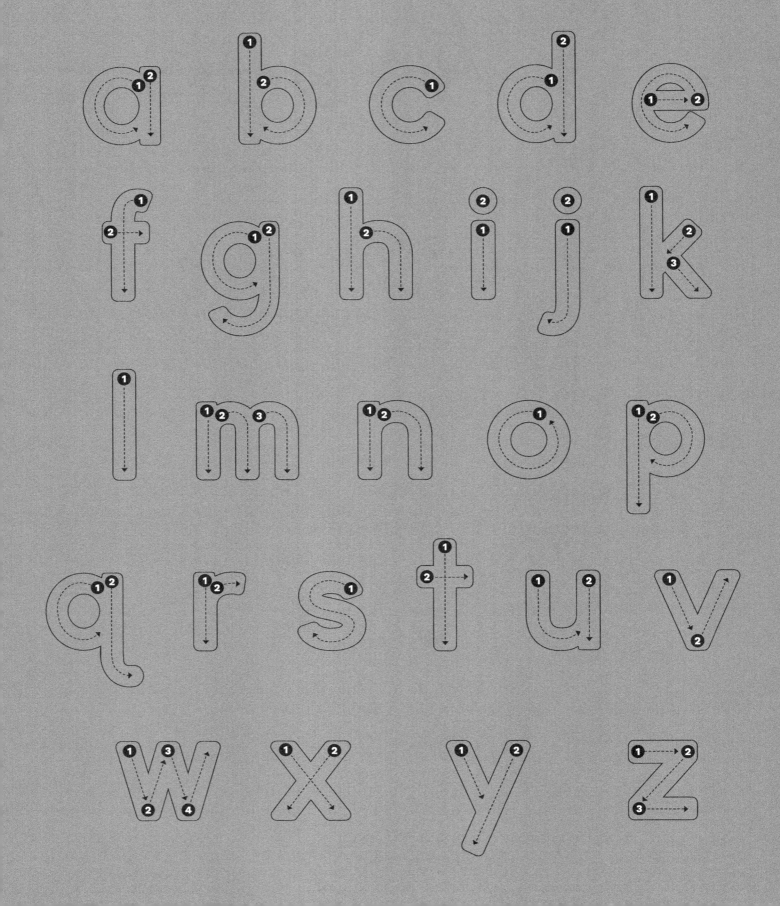

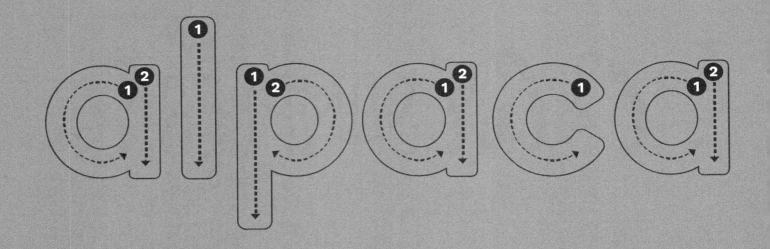

animal facts

Alpaca's teeth are designed for efficient feeding. They grab grass, shut their mouth on it and press the grass against a special dental pad at the front of their top jaw with their incisors.

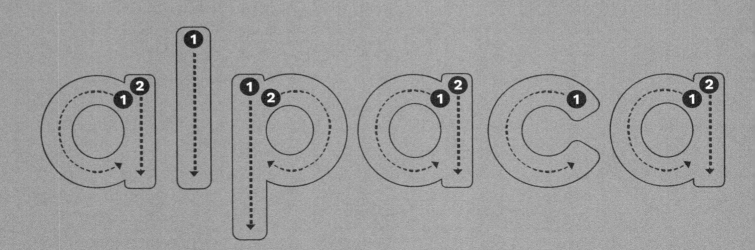

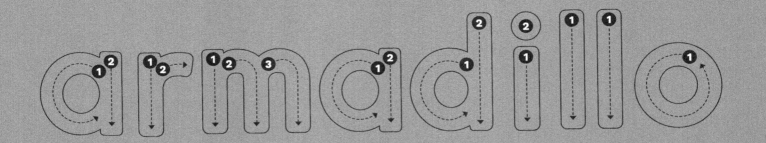

animal facts

Armadillos are
barrel-shaped animals
covered with natural
armor. In fact, its name in
Spanish means "little
armored one"

animal facts

Butterflies have four wings,
not two as you may think.
They have been around for
over 56 million years.
Butterflies have four stages
in their life cycle: egg,
larvae, pupa, and adult.

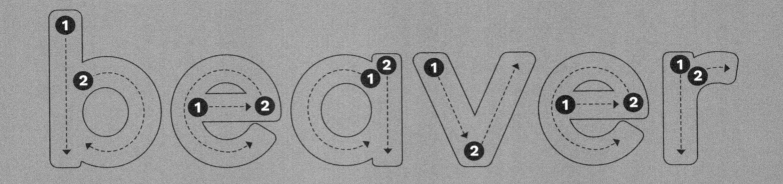

animal facts

Beavers are one of the
largest rodents on earth,
their teeth never stop
growing, so they are
always gnawing on wood to
keep them from
growing too long

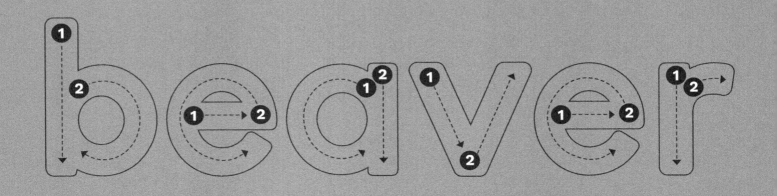

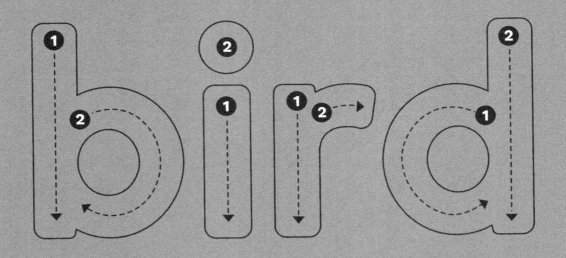

animal facts

The largest living bird in the world is the Ostrich and the smallest is the Hummingbird.

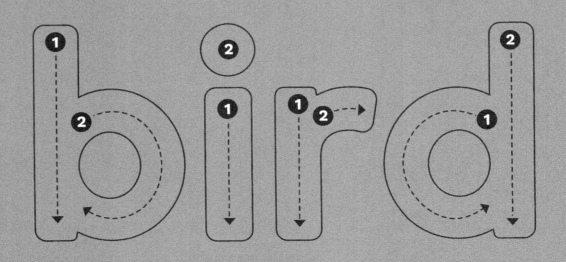

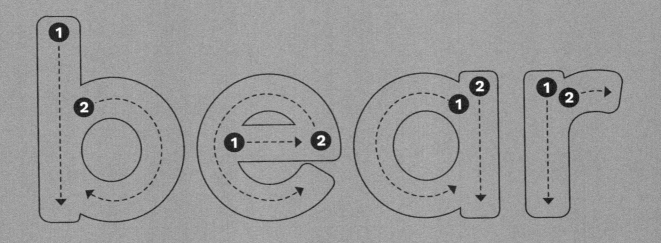

animal facts

Bears eat mostly meat and
fish, but some bears also
eat plants and insects.

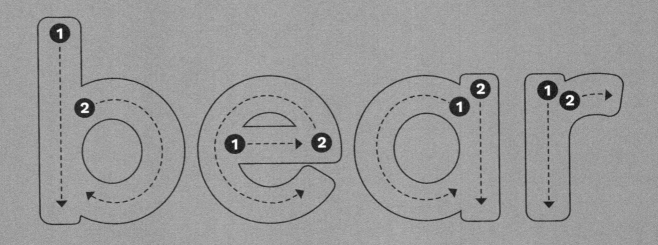

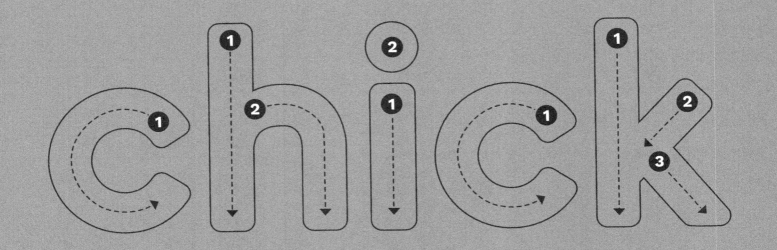

animal facts

Baby chickens are chicks.
Female chickens are pullets
until they're old enough to
lay eggs and become hens.

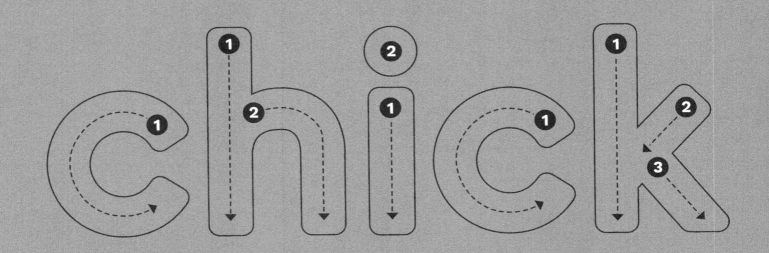

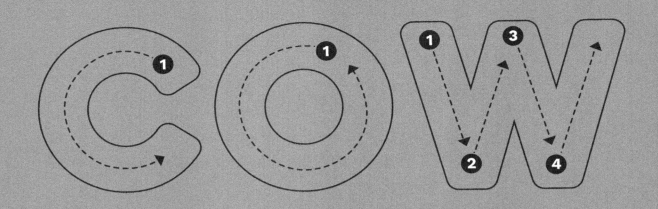

animal facts

A cow will chew about 50
times in a minute,
making their jaws move
about 40,000 times a day.

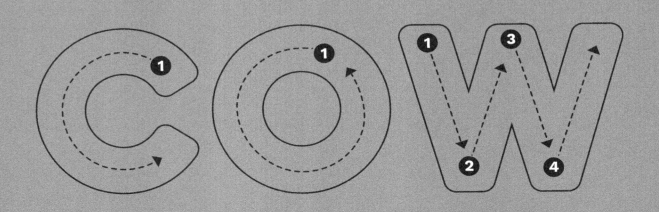

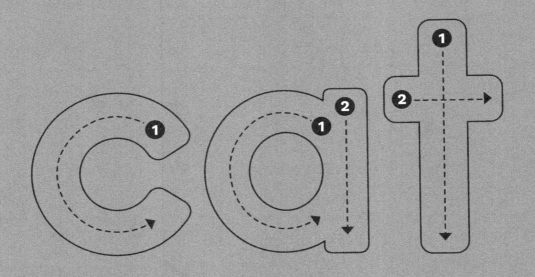

animal facts

The hearing of the average cat is at least five times better than a human adult.

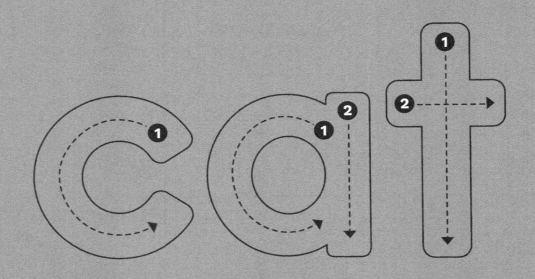

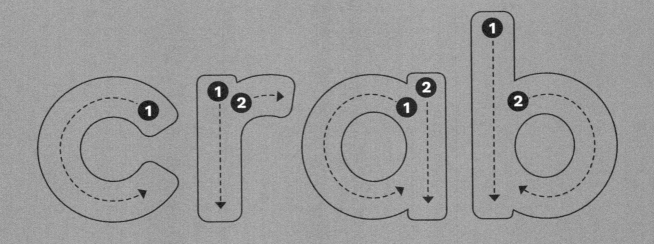

animal facts

There are more than 4,500
species of crabs.
Most species live in
coastal areas of salty, fresh
or brackish water.

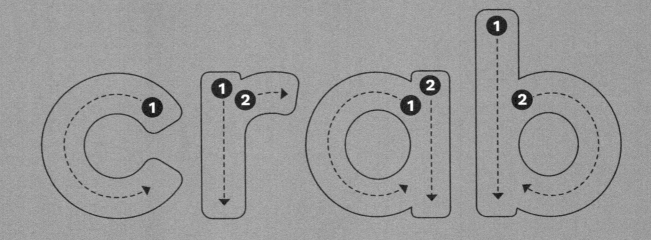

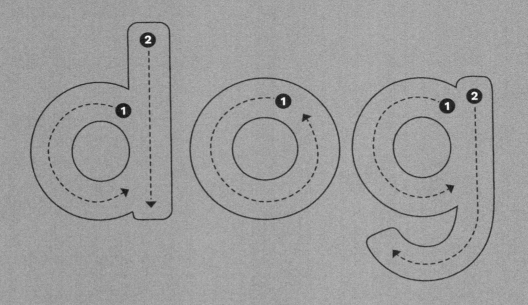

animal facts

Dog's sense of smell is at least 40 times better than ours. Dogs have the ability to breathe and sniff at the same time.

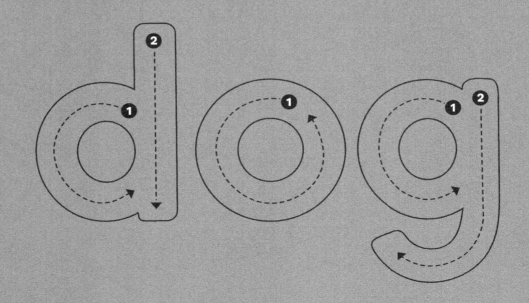

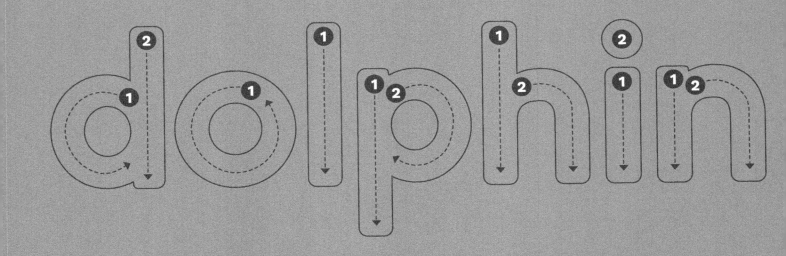

animal facts

Dolphins are marine
mammals. They must
surface to breathe air and
give birth to live young.

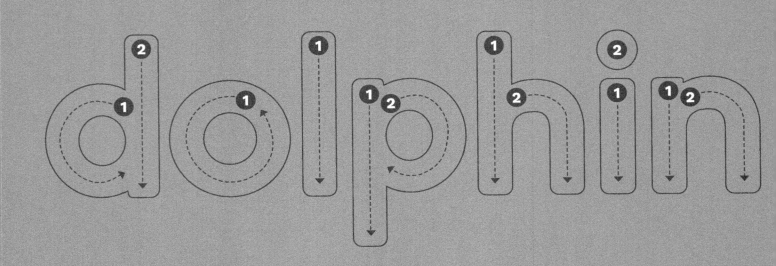

animal facts

Having a dragonfly land on your head is considered good luck. Dragonflies like to live in warm climates and near the water.

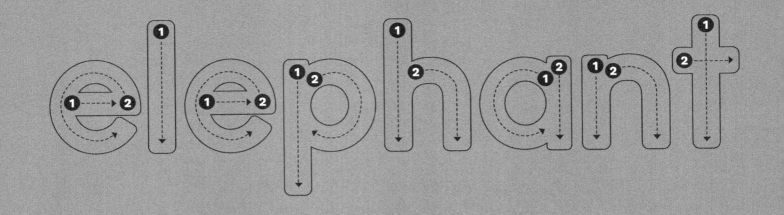

animal facts

The African elephant is the world's largest land mammal, with males on average measuring up to 10 feet high and weighing up to 6 tonnes.

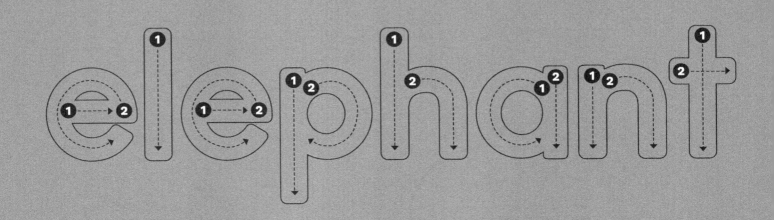

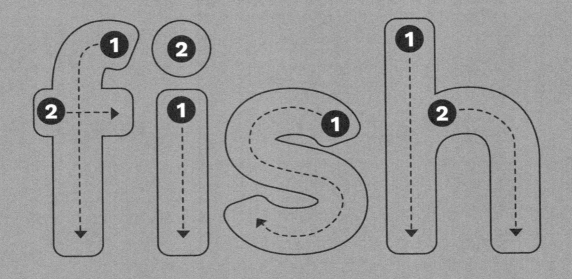

animal facts

Fish have a specialised sense
organ called their lateral
line, it's like a radar and helps
them navigate in dark or
murky water.

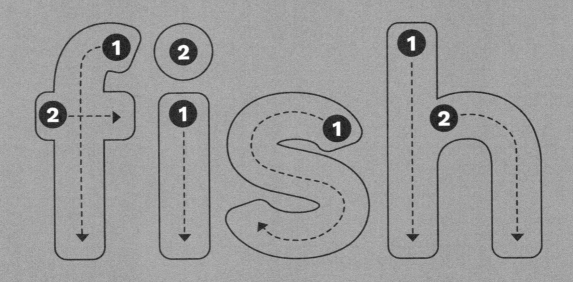

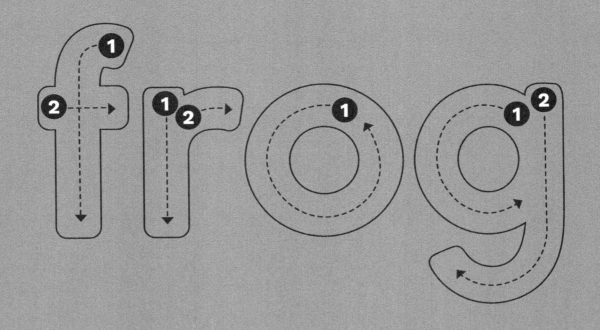

animal facts

Frogs are found all over the
world and they drink water
through their skin.
A group of frogs is called an
army.

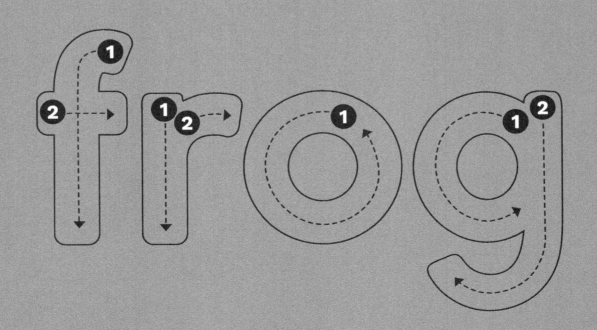

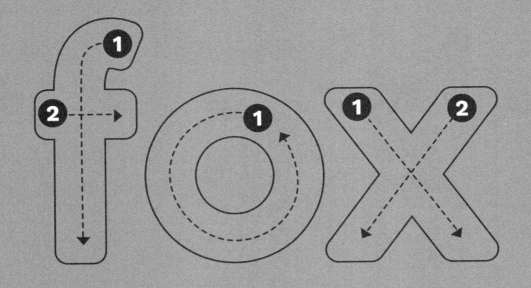

animal facts

Foxes live in dens in the ground or old trees. One female fox is the boss. She is the only one in her area that has babies. The other adult foxes help her raise the pups.

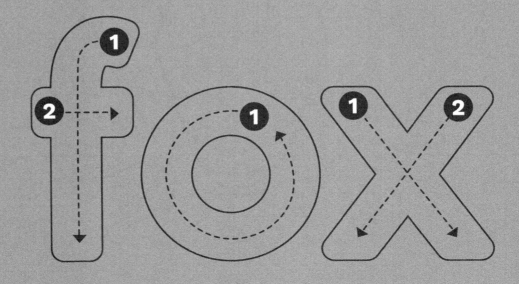

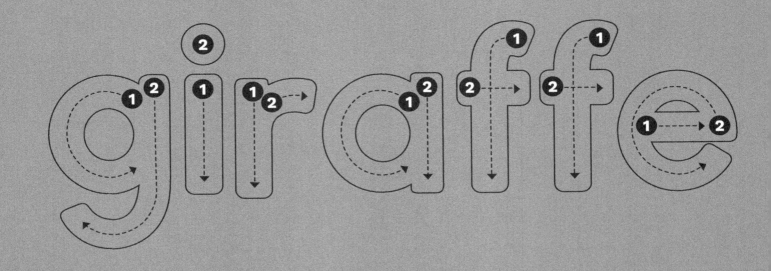

animal facts

Giraffes sleep only five to 30 minutes every day. Usually they stand up to sleep. They only lie down if another giraffe can stand watch.

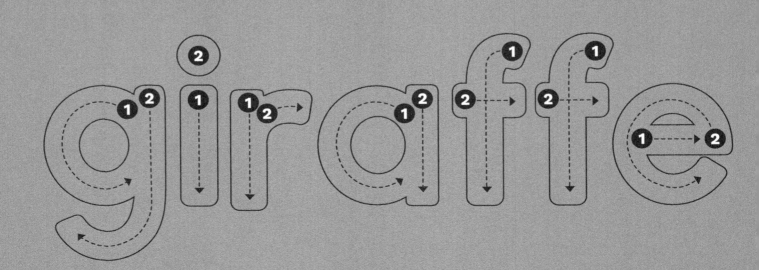

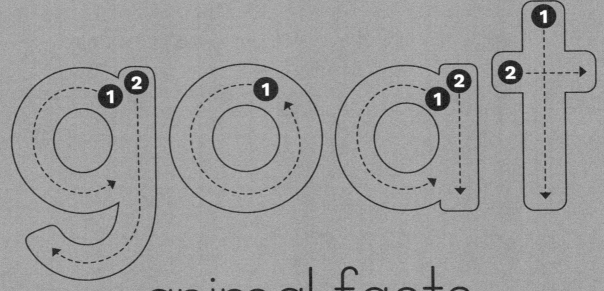

animal facts

Baby goats stand and start taking their first steps within minutes of being born. Each baby goat has a unique call and scent, that is how its mother recognizes it from birth, not by sight.

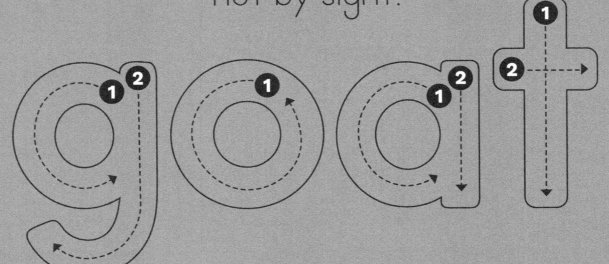

animal facts

Gazelles are relatively small
antelopes,they tend to live
in herds, and eat less coarse,
easily digestible plants and
leaves.

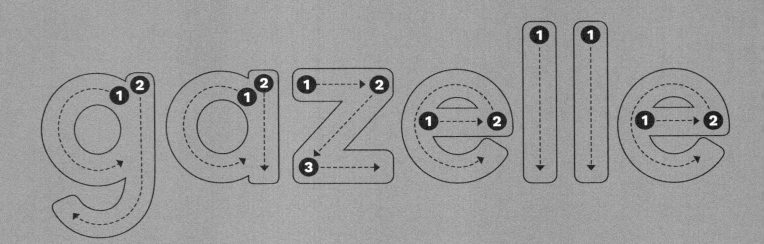

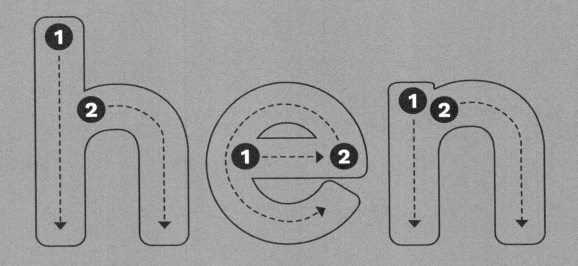

animal facts

Female chickens are pullets until they're old enough to lay eggs and become hens. There are more chickens on earth than people, there are also more chickens than any other bird species

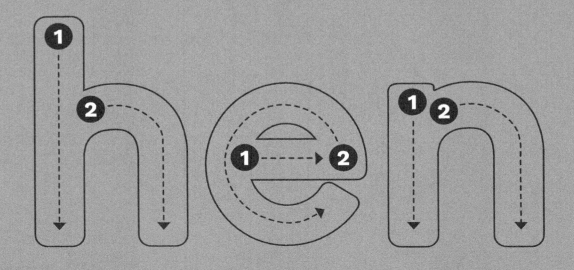

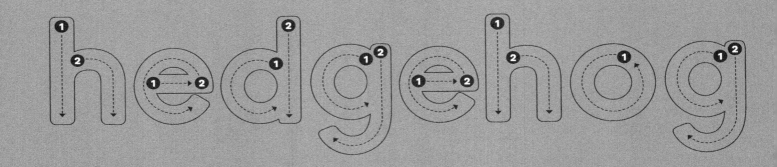

animal facts

The "Hedge" part of their
name comes from where
they build their nests
hedges, bushes and shrubs.
The "hog" part comes from
the small snorting
sound they make which is
similar to a pig or warthog.

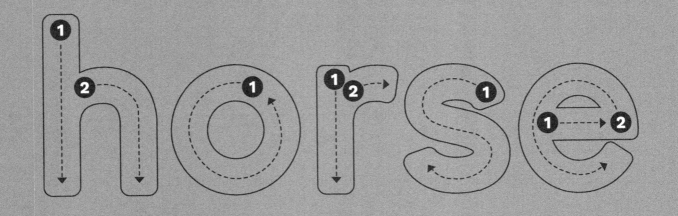

animal facts

Horses can run shortly
after birth and they can
sleep both lying down and
standing up. Horses have
bigger eyes than any other
mammal that lives on land.

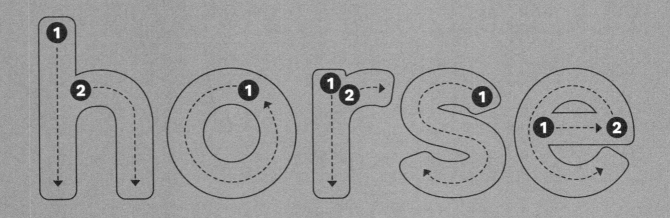

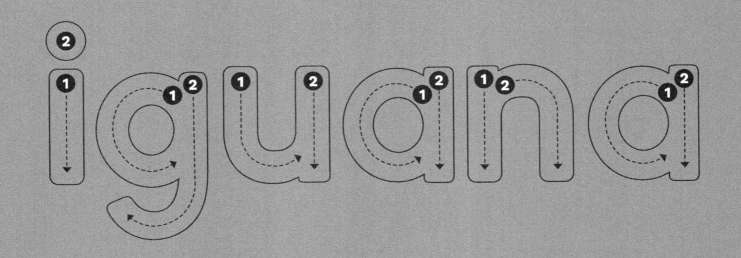

animal facts

Iguanas are very large
lizards that can live 20 or
more years and can grow
as long as 6 feet. More than
half of their body length is
due to their
long tail.

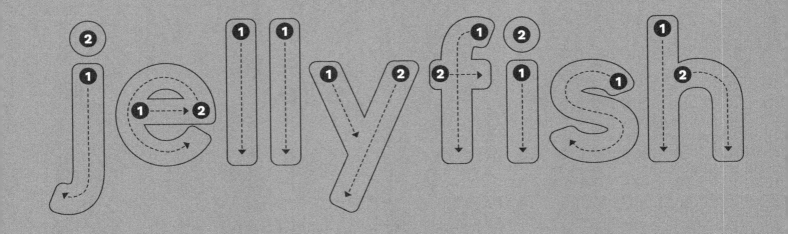

animal facts

Some jellyfish can glow in
the dark because they have
bioluminescent
organs which emit blue or
green light.

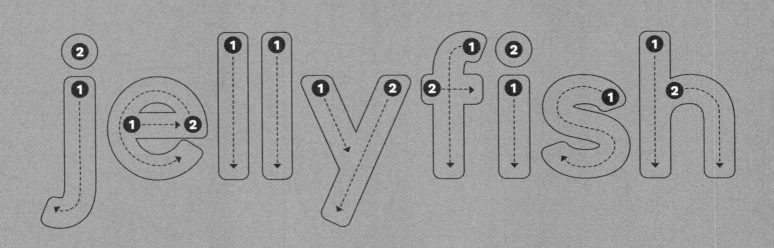

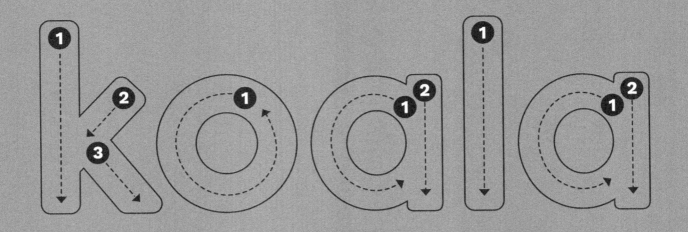

animal facts

Koalas are often referred
to as Koala Bears, but
they're actually marsupials
not bears, they live in
eucalypt forests and eat
gum leaves which are
usually toxic to other
animals.

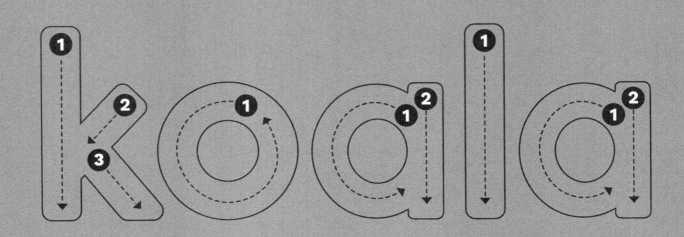

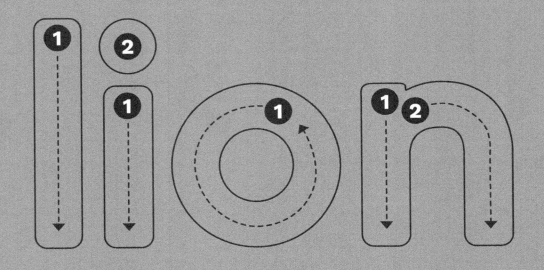

animal facts

Lions belong to the big cat family and are the second largest big cat in the world after the tiger. Lions, like pet cats, can be very lazy creatures, spending around 20 hours a day resting.

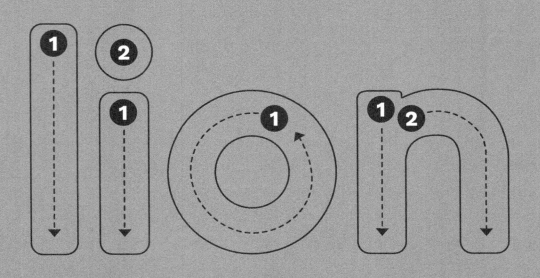

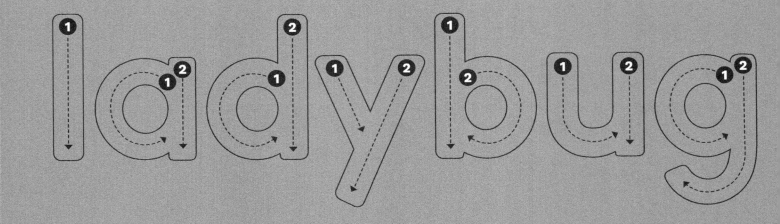

animal facts

Depending on the species, ladybugs can have spots, stripes, or no markings at all. Ladybugs are happy in many different habitats, including grasslands, forests, cities, suburbs, and along rivers.

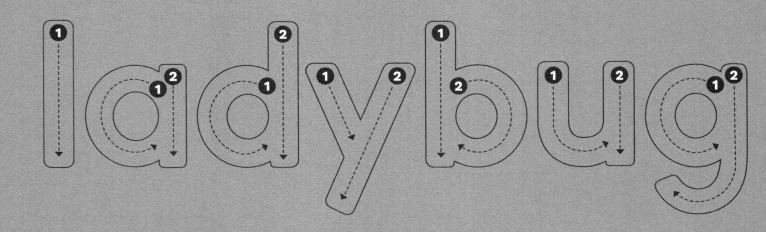

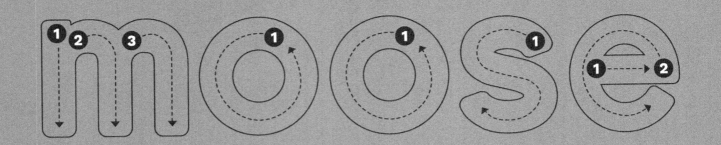

animal facts

Moose usually live in areas with cold, snowy winters, including North America, Europe and Asia. Moose like to swim. They can swim many miles without stopping and can stay underwater for up to 30 seconds.

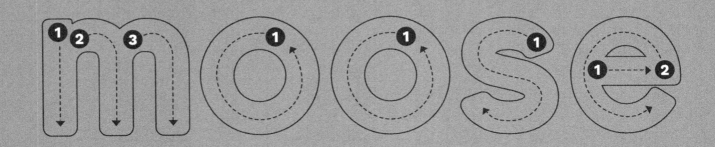

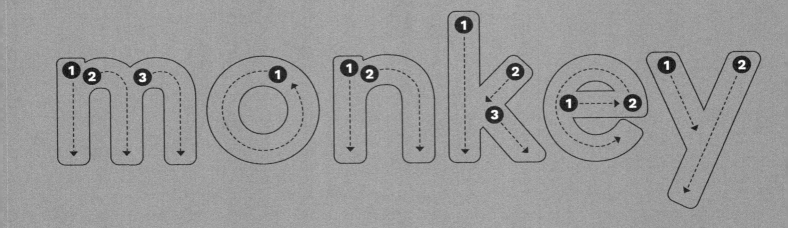

animal facts

Monkey is a common name
for a group of primate
mammals. There are over
260 different species of
monkeys worldwide.

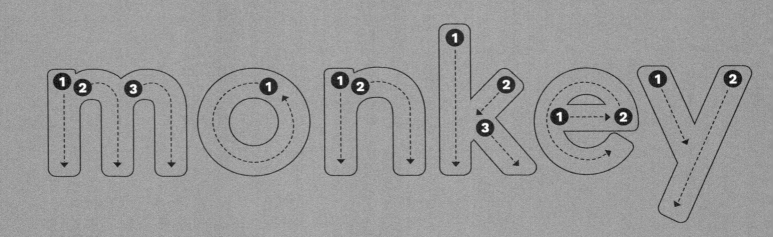

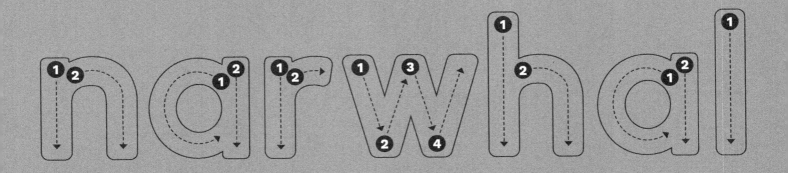

animal facts

A narwhal is a
medium-sized toothed
whale that has a large "tusk"
from a sticking
canine tooth. Narwhals can
live up to 50 years.

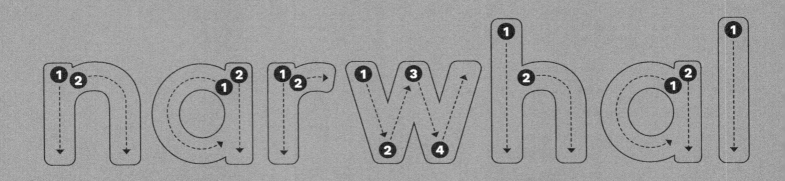

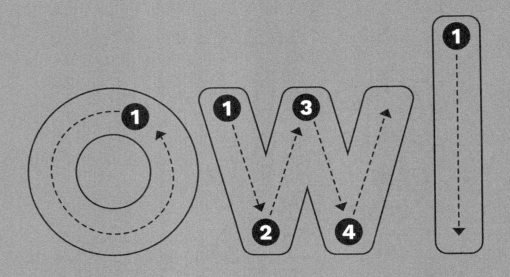

animal facts

Owls can't move their eyes.
They must turn their heads
to see and they can turn
their heads almost
completely around.

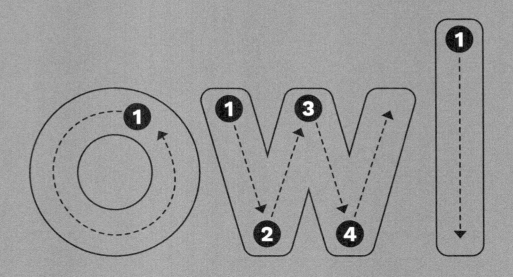

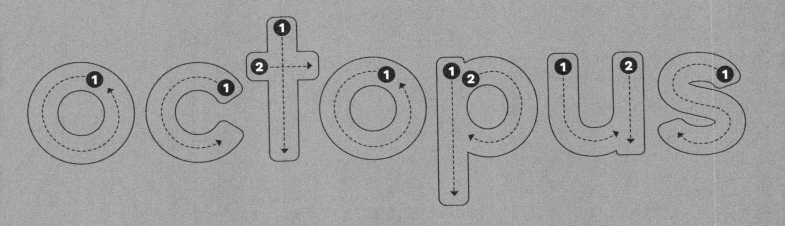

animal facts

Most octopuses stay along
the ocean's floor, although
some species are "pelagic,"
meaning they live near the
water's surface.

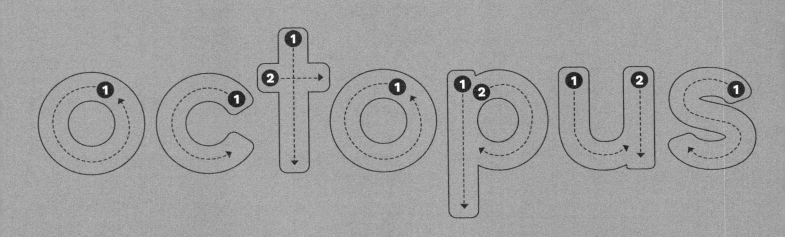

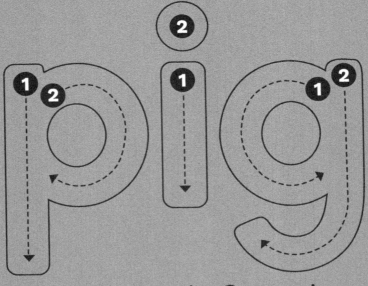

animal facts

Pigs are intelligent animals. A pig's snout is an important tool for finding food in the ground and sensing the world around them. Pigs have an excellent sense of smell.

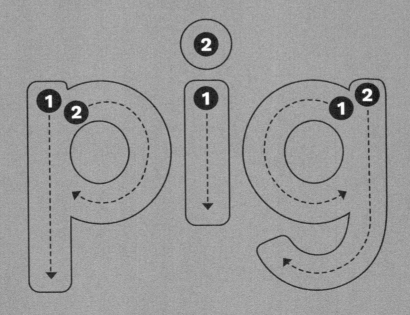

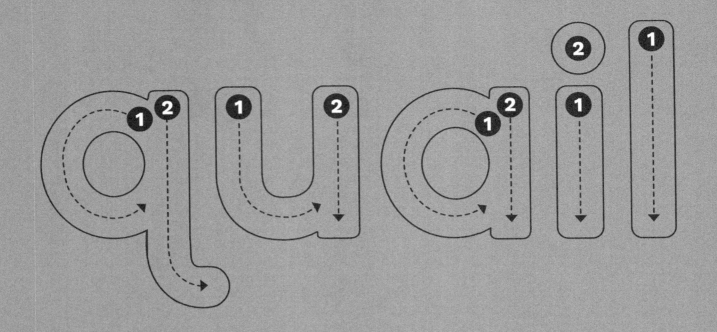

animal facts

Quails eat seeds, grain and insects and can lay 10 to 20 eggs at one time.

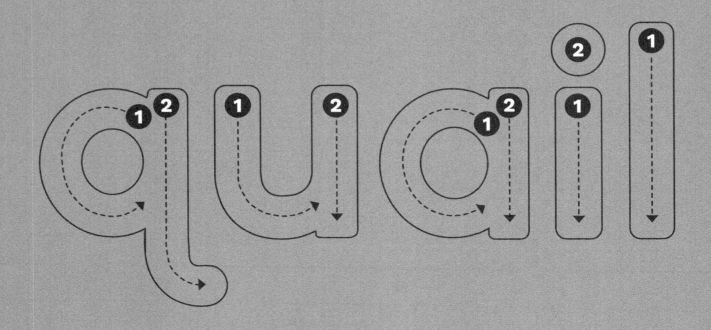

animal facts

Roosters are protectors. A
good rooster will take this
duty seriously and keep an
eye out for trouble
at all times.

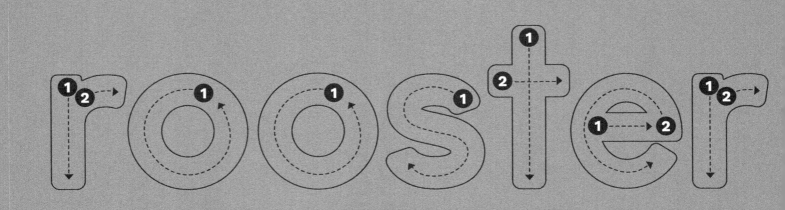

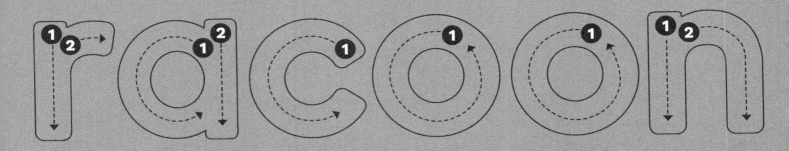

animal facts

Raccoons are omnivores,
they eat almost anything!
They are nocturnal,
meaning they are awake
during the night and sleep in
the day.

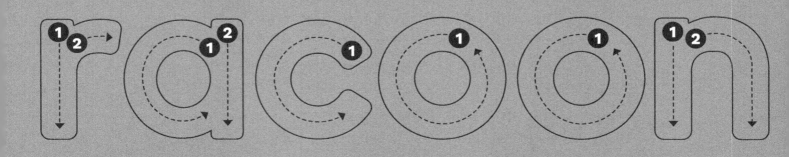

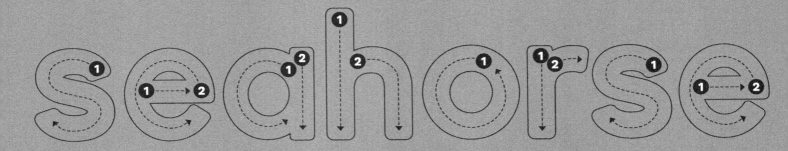

animal facts

A seahorses tail can grasp
objects, which comes in
handy when they want to
anchor themselves to
vegetation.

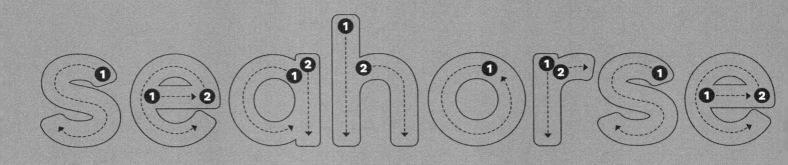

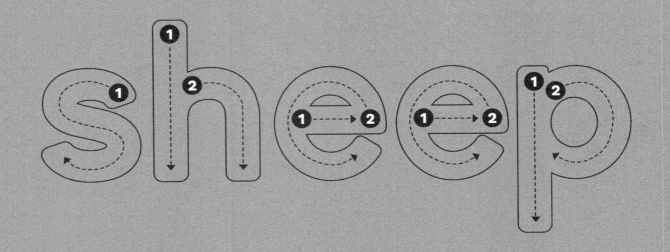

animal facts

Sheep have a groove in their upper lip that divides it in half, this groove is called a philtrum.
Sheep are highly social and smart animals.

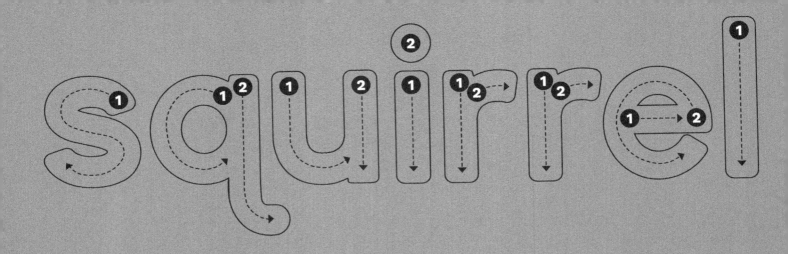

animal facts

Squirrels are rodents.
Most squirrels are small and
have big eyes and bushy
tails, they eat mostly nuts,
fruits and seeds.

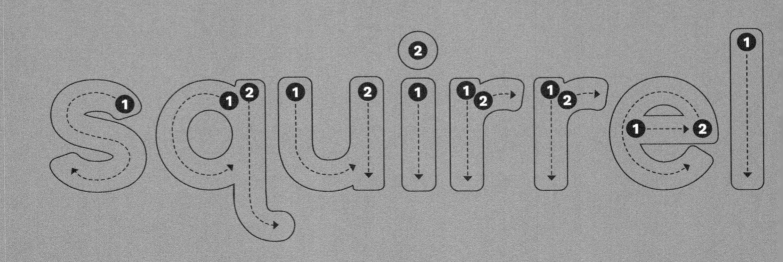

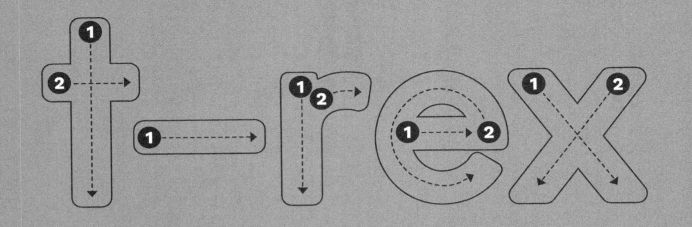

animal facts

Tyrannosaurus Rex had powerful back legs that let it hunt prey over short distances at up to 20mph. They lived about 65 to 70 million years ago – in the late cretaceous period.

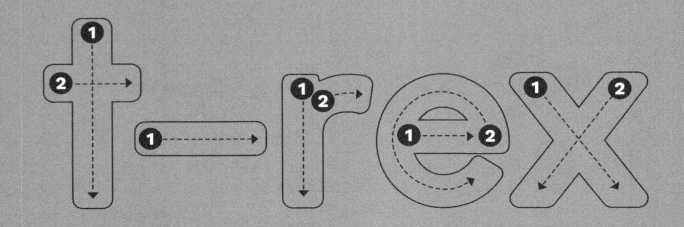

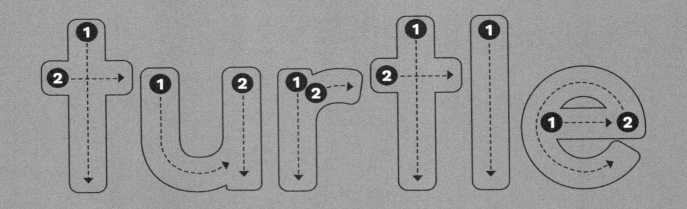

animal facts

Turtles date back to the
time of the dinosaurs, over
200 million years ago!
Their shell acts like a shield
to protect them from
predators.

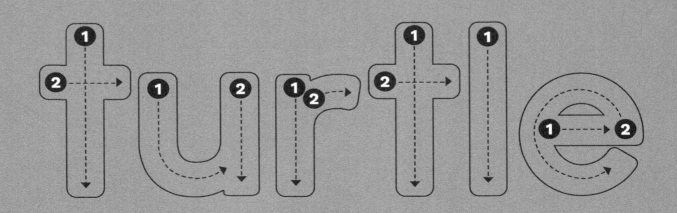

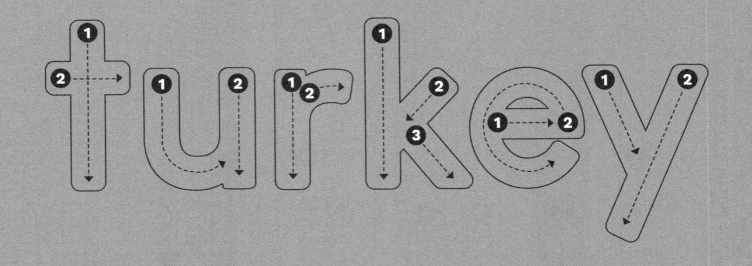

animal facts

Wild Turkeys spend their
days looking for and eating
food such as acorns, seeds,
small insects, berries, and
fruits.

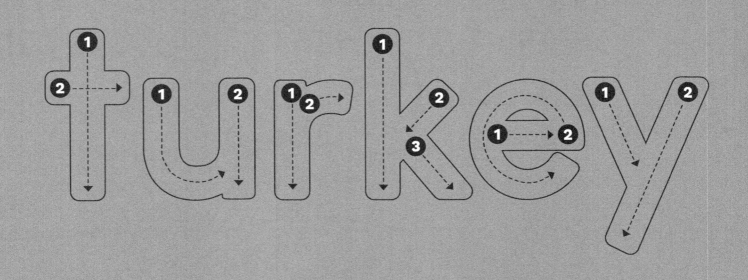

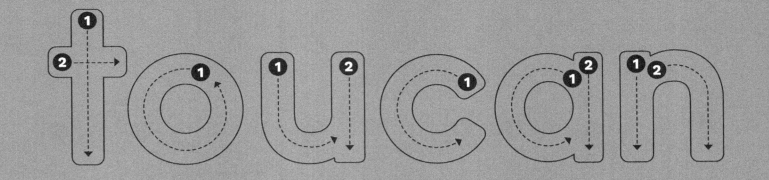

animal facts

Toucans can be found in the
tropical forests of South
America, and can also find
homes in tree
hollows or abandoned
woodpecker holes.

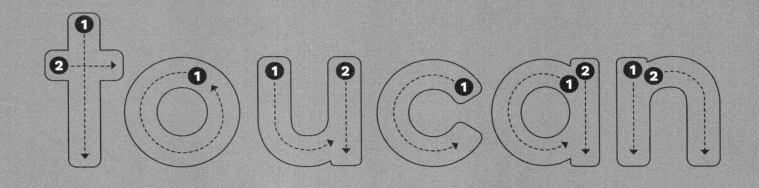

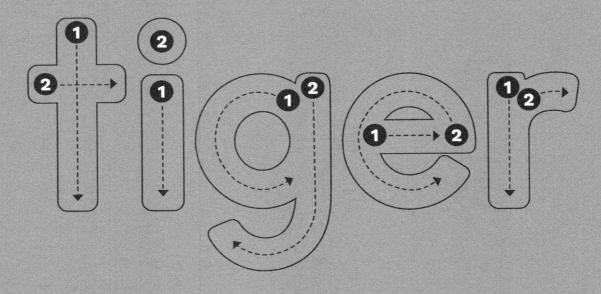

animal facts

Unlike most members of the cat family, tigers seem to enjoy water and swim well. A tiger knows if it is in another tiger's territory based on the trees around him.

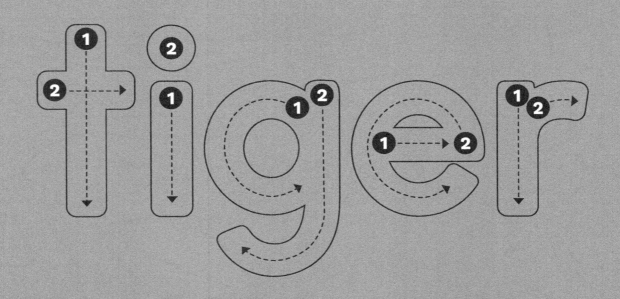

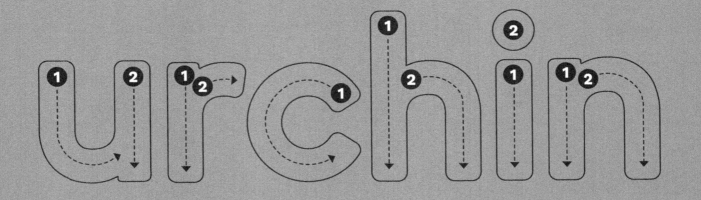

animal facts

Sea urchins are
covered with long, movable
spines. These spines help
the slow-moving animal to
"walk" and are also used to
keep away enemies.

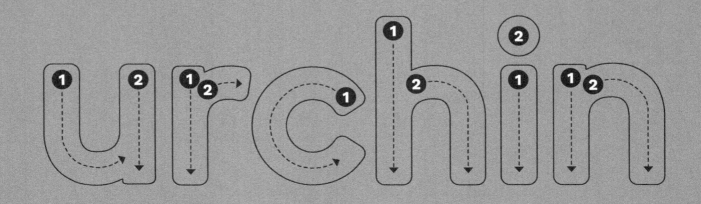

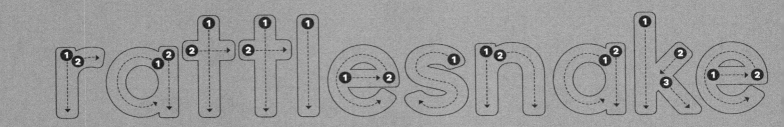

animal facts

As rattlesnakes age,
segments on the end of the
rattle wear out and break
off. New segments grow
when the rattlesnake sheds
its skin, or molts.

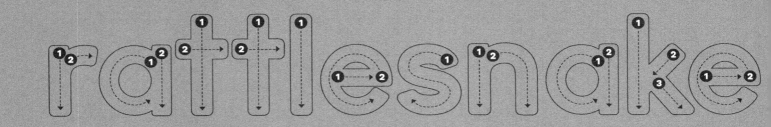

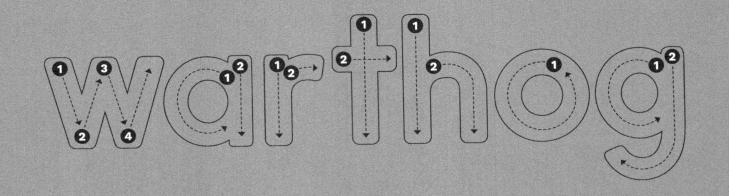

animal facts

Most warthogs like to look
for food during the light of
the morning and early
evening. But if they live in an
area where they are
hunted by people, they
switch to foraging
at night.

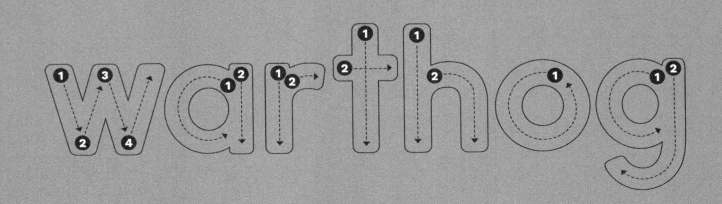

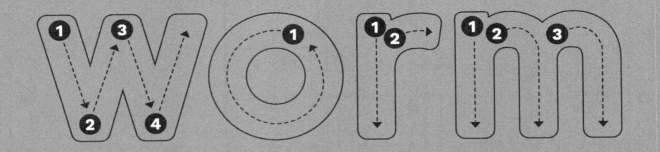

animal facts

Worms live where there is
food, moisture, oxygen and
a favorable temperature.
If they don't have these
things, they go somewhere
else.

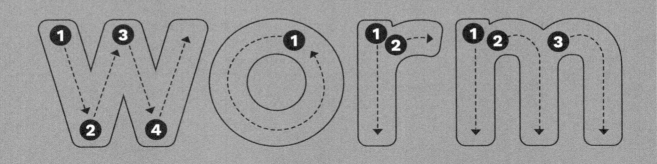

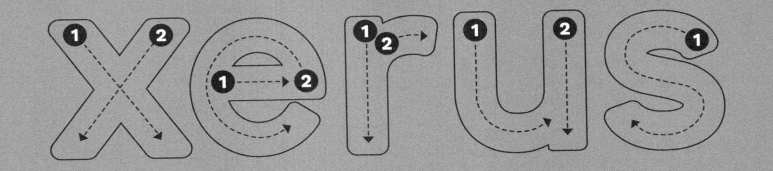

animal facts

The Xerus is also known as
the African Ground
Squirrel. They eat roots,
seeds, fruits, grains,
insects, small vertebrates
and eggs.

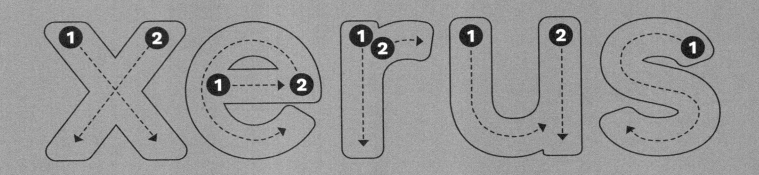

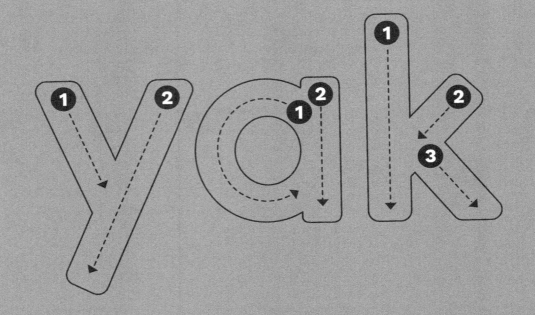

animal facts

Yaks originate in the
Himalayan Mountains.
They have great balance
and never fall down.

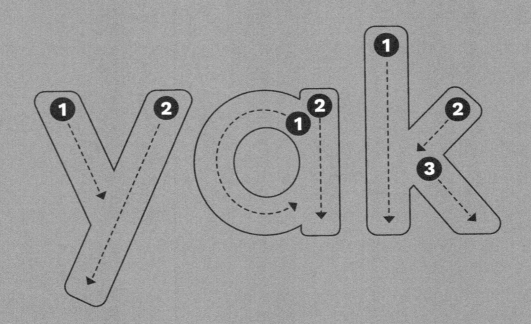

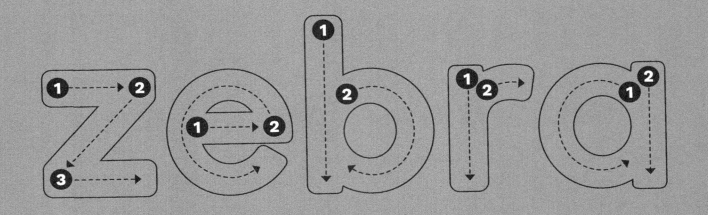

animal facts

Closely related to
horses, zebras have thick
bodies, thin legs, a
tufted tail, and a long head.
But their most famous
feature is the black and
white striped coat.

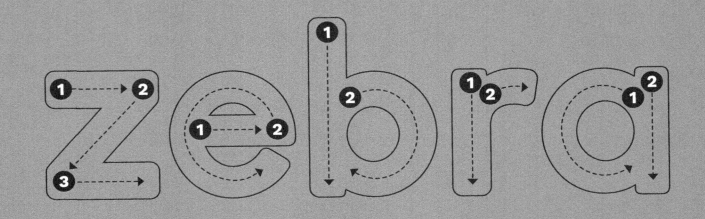

about the author

Hola! My name is Joy Kelley, I was born in Chile, but I currently reside in the Mountains of Southern California.

I am the mom of 3 little boys and a proud fire wife obsessed with lemon pie. While my degree is in Industrial Design, I have been a full-time lettering artist since 2013.

I have been fortunate to work on fun lettering and calligraphy projects for my shop and design studio (howjoyfulshop.com and howjoyfulstudio.com) and as a freelancer with small and big clients doing branding, editorial, and licensing projects. My work has been featured in publications such as People Magazine, The Today Show, and Project Nursery. I've had my artwork with products for sale nationwide in stores like Nordstrom and TJ-Maxx.

Out of everything I do, teaching lettering, calligraphy, and sharing my love for all things creative is what brings me the most joy and fulfillment. So, If you are interested in those kinds of resources, you can find a lot of free content on my blog (howjoyful.com).

I sincerely hope that your little one has as much fun coloring as I did drawing these pages, along with my little ones =]

Joy Kelley

FIND ME ONLINE
@howjoyful

my books!

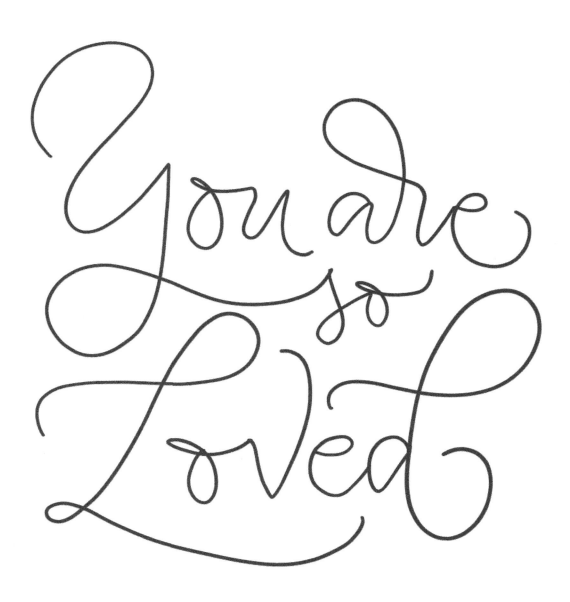

CONNER, COLLIN, AND COOPER.
MAY THE COLORS OF YOUR LIFE ALWAYS BE BRIGHT.

Made in the USA
Middletown, DE
25 September 2023

39172200R00064